DATE NIGHT DECADENCE

DATE NIGHT DECADENCE

NIGEL WEBER

ZG Book Publishing, California.

Printed in the United States of America
First Printing, July 2023

In the end, only three things matter: how much you loved, how gently you lived, and how gracefully you let go of things not meant for you.

—BUDDHA

TABLE OF CONTENTS

APPETIZER

Golden and crisp risotto, filled with melted mozzarella and served with a rich tomato sauce, these Italian-style bite-sized delights bring elegance and decadence to your date night.

ARANCINI

2	cups of leftover risotto, cooled
1/2	cup of mozzarella, cut into small cubes
1	cup of all-purpose flour
2	large eggs, beaten
1	cup of breadcrumbs
2	cups of marinara sauce, for dipping
	Vegetable oil, for frying
	Fresh basil leaves, for garnish

Prep Time: 15 minutes
Cook Time: 15 minutes
Total Time: 30 minutes
Servings: 4 (around 16 arancini)

Take a small amount of the risotto in your hand and flatten it out. Place a cube of mozzarella in the center, then roll the risotto around the cheese to form a ball. Repeat with the rest of the risotto and mozzarella. Roll each risotto ball first in flour, then dip in the beaten egg, and finally roll in breadcrumbs to coat evenly.

Heat the vegetable oil in a deep frying pan over medium-high heat. Once hot, fry the risotto balls in batches, turning occasionally, until golden brown and crispy, about 4-5 minutes. Use a slotted spoon to transfer the arancini to a paper towel-lined plate to drain excess oil.

Warm the marinara sauce in a small saucepan or in the microwave. Serve the hot arancini with the warmed marinara sauce for dipping, garnish with fresh basil leaves.

Wine Pairing:
A medium-bodied Italian red, such as a Chianti or a Montepulciano, would pair beautifully with these arancini. The wine's acidity and tannins balance the richness of the risotto balls, and its earthy notes complement the tomato sauce. If you prefer white wine, a Vermentino or a Soave could be a great choice. Their crisp acidity can cut through the richness of the dish, while the citrus notes add a refreshing contrast.

The combination of the chewy dates, crunchy almonds, and crispy bacon creates an unforgettable flavor experience.

BACON-WRAPPED DATES STUFFED WITH ALMONDS

16   pitted dates
16   whole almonds
8   slices of bacon, cut in half
16   toothpicks
      Balsamic glaze, for drizzling

Prep Time: 10 minutes
Cook Time: 20 minutes
Total Time: 30 minutes
Servings: 4 (makes 16)

Preheat your oven to 375°F (190°C) and line a baking sheet with parchment paper. Stuff each date with an almond and then wrap with a half slice of bacon, securing with a toothpick.

Place the wrapped dates on the prepared baking sheet, making sure they are spaced apart. Bake for 15-20 minutes, or until the bacon is crisp. Be sure to turn the dates halfway through the cooking time to ensure even crisping.

Allow the dates to cool slightly before serving, as the filling will be hot. Finish with the balsamic glaze.

Note: This recipe is incredibly versatile. Add goat or blue cheese for added depth of flavor. Try a variety of nut and cheese combinations to keep this dish fresh and creative.

Wine Pairing:
A slightly off-dry and fruity rosé will perfectly complement the sweet dates and salty bacon. The wine's light body and delicate flavors won't overpower the dish, while its hint of sweetness can match the dates' natural sugars. If you prefer red wine, opt for a light-bodied and fruity Pinot Noir. Its bright acidity can cut through the bacon's richness, and its subtle earthy notes can enhance the dish's savory elements.

The delicate, mildly spicy shishito peppers become wonderfully smoky when charred, and the savory soy glaze adds the perfect finishing touch.

CHARRED SHISHITO PEPPERS WITH SOY GLAZE

1	pound shishito peppers	Prep Time: 5 minutes
1	tablespoon olive oil	Cook Time: 10 minutes
1/4	cup soy sauce	Total Time: 15 minutes
2	tablespoons honey	Servings: 4
1	tablespoon rice vinegar	
1	tablespoon toasted sesame seeds	

Preheat a large skillet or grill pan over medium-high heat. Toss the shishito peppers with the olive oil and add to the hot pan. Cook, turning occasionally, until the peppers are blistered and charred, about 5-7 minutes.

Meanwhile, combine the soy sauce, honey, and rice vinegar in a small saucepan over medium heat. Stir until the honey is dissolved and the mixture is heated through. Transfer the charred peppers to a serving dish. Drizzle with the warm soy glaze and sprinkle with the toasted sesame seeds.

Wine Pairing:
A vibrant, medium-bodied white wine like a Grüner Veltliner would make a delightful companion for this dish. Its lively acidity and peppery notes can balance the shishito peppers' mild heat, while its citrusy undertones can complement the soy glaze's umami flavors. If you prefer a more fruit-forward wine, a well-chilled rosé with notes of strawberry and cherry would also work beautifully.

Clams Casino is a delightful seafood appetizer that's sure to impress. Fresh clams are topped with a mouthwatering mixture of crispy bacon, bell peppers, and bread crumbs, then broiled to perfection. Served with a squeeze of fresh lemon, it's a wonderful start to a memorable meal.

CLAMS CASINO

24	littleneck clams
6	slices of bacon, chopped
1/2	cup bell peppers, finely chopped
1/2	cup onion, finely chopped
3	cloves of garlic, minced
1/2	cup bread crumbs
1/4	cup Parmesan cheese, grated
2	tablespoons of olive oil
2	tablespoons fresh parsley, chopped
	Salt and pepper to taste
	Lemon wedges for serving

Prep Time: 20 minutes
Cook Time: 10 minutes
Total Time: 30 minutes
Servings: 4

Preheat your oven's broiler. Clean the clams and open them, discarding the top shell. Arrange them on a baking sheet.

In a skillet, cook the bacon over medium heat until crisp. Remove and drain on paper towels. In the same skillet, add the bell peppers, onion, and garlic. Sauté until soft, about 5 minutes.

In a bowl, combine the cooked vegetables, bacon, bread crumbs, Parmesan cheese, salt, and pepper. Drizzle with olive oil and mix until well combined. Top each clam with the mixture, ensuring each is well covered.

Broil in the preheated oven until the topping is golden and sizzling, about 5-7 minutes. Be sure to watch them closely to prevent burning. Garnish with fresh parsley and serve with lemon wedges on the side.

Wine Pairing:
Pair with a crisp, mineral-driven white wine like a Vermentino or a Sancerre. The wine's acidity and citrus notes will complement the brininess of the clams and the crisp, savory topping. If you prefer a fuller-bodied wine, a Chardonnay with a moderate amount of oak could also work well with this dish.

These irresistible Crab Cakes, served with a tangy Remoulade Sauce, are perfectly seasoned, full of succulent crab meat, and pan-seared until golden brown. Serve with a creamy, flavor-packed sauce for dipping on the side.

CRAB CAKES WITH REMOULADE SAUCE

FOR THE CRAB CAKES:

Prep Time: 15 minutes
Cook Time: 10 minutes
Total Time: 25 minutes
Servings: 4

1	pound lump crab meat, picked over for shells
1/2	cup panko bread crumbs
1/4	cup mayonnaise
1	egg, lightly beaten
1	tablespoon Dijon mustard
1	tablespoon fresh parsley, chopped
1/2	teaspoon Old Bay seasoning
1/4	teaspoon salt
2	tablespoons olive oil

FOR THE REMOULADE SAUCE:

1/2	cup mayonnaise
2	tablespoons capers, drained and chopped
1	tablespoon Dijon mustard
1	tablespoon fresh lemon juice
1	clove garlic, minced
1	teaspoon hot sauce
1/2	teaspoon paprika

In a large bowl, combine crab meat, panko, mayonnaise, egg, Dijon mustard, parsley, Old Bay seasoning, and salt. Mix gently until well combined. Shape the mixture into 8 cakes about 1 inch thick.

Heat the olive oil in a large skillet over medium heat. Add the crab cakes to the skillet and cook until golden brown and crisp, about 3-4 minutes per side.

For the Remoulade Sauce, whisk together mayonnaise, capers, Dijon mustard, lemon juice, garlic, hot sauce, and paprika until smooth. Serve the crab cakes hot with Remoulade Sauce on the side.

Wine Pairing:
A Sauvignon Blanc with its high acidity and citrus notes, or a Chardonnay with minimal oak, would pair beautifully with the crab and the tangy Remoulade Sauce.

GAZPACHO SHOOTERS

1	pound ripe tomatoes, cored and roughly chopped
1	red bell pepper, seeded and roughly chopped
1	cucumber, peeled, seeded and roughly chopped
1	small red onion, peeled and roughly chopped
1	clove garlic, peeled
2	tablespoons sherry vinegar
1/3	cup extra-virgin olive oil
	Salt, to taste
	Freshly ground black pepper, to taste
	Chopped fresh parsley, for garnish

Prep Time: 15 minutes
Chilling Time: 2 hours
Total Time: 2 hours
and 15 minutes
Servings: 4

In a blender or food processor, combine the tomatoes, bell pepper, cucumber, red onion, garlic, and sherry vinegar. Blend until smooth. While the blender is running, slowly add the olive oil until it's fully incorporated into the soup. Season the gazpacho with salt and pepper to taste. Pour the soup through a fine-mesh sieve into a large bowl, pressing on the solids with a spatula to extract as much liquid as possible. Discard the solids. Cover the bowl with plastic wrap and chill the gazpacho in the refrigerator for at least 2 hours, or until it's thoroughly cold.

To serve, pour the gazpacho into shot glasses, garnish with chopped fresh parsley, and serve immediately.

These Mini Beef Wellingtons deliver all the flavors of the classic dish but in a more personal and playful form. Tender pieces of filet mignon are seared, then coated in a rich mushroom duxelles, wrapped in prosciutto, and finally encased in a golden puff pastry shell, resulting in an irresistibly elegant dish.

MINI BEEF WELLINGTONS

2	filet mignon steaks (6 oz. each)
8	slices of prosciutto
8 oz	button mushrooms, finely chopped
2	tablespoons of olive oil
1	small shallot, finely chopped
2	cloves garlic, minced
1	sheet of puff pastry, thawed
1	egg (for egg wash)
1	tablespoon of Dijon mustard
	Salt and pepper to taste

Prep Time: 25 minutes
Cook Time: 20 minutes
Total Time: 45 minutes
Servings: 4

Preheat the oven to 400°F (200°C). Cut the filets in half, season with salt and pepper. Heat 1 tablespoon of oil in a skillet over high heat. Sear the filets on all sides until browned, about 2 minutes per side. Remove the filets from the pan and let them cool.

In the same pan, add the remaining oil, then add the shallots, garlic, and chopped mushrooms. Season with salt and pepper. Cook over medium heat until the mushrooms are golden and all the liquid has evaporated. Let this mushroom mixture (duxelles) cool.

Spread out the prosciutto slices on a clean surface, slightly overlapping. Spread half the duxelles over the prosciutto. Brush each mini steak with the Dijon mustard and the four mini steaks on the prosciutto and duxelles. Roll up the prosciutto around each steak to fully encase it. Cut the puff pastry into 4 squares. Place the wrapped steak on a pastry square. Fold the pastry over the steak, sealing it with a bit of beaten egg. Repeat with the remaining steaks. Place the wrapped steaks on a baking sheet and brush with the beaten egg to create an egg wash.

Bake in the preheated oven for about 20 minutes or until the pastry is golden brown. Let the mini Beef Wellingtons rest for 5 minutes before serving to ensure the juices are evenly distributed.

Wine Pairing:
A medium-bodied red wine, like a Pinot Noir, will complement the richness of the beef and the earthy mushroom duxelles without overpowering the dish.

Delicate, savory, and just the right amount of sweet, these Parmesan Shortbreads topped with fresh figs are the perfect way to start any meal on a high note. Perfectly buttery with a hint of Parmesan flavor, they pair beautifully with the sweetness of figs.

Parmesan Shortbread with Figs

FOR THE SHORTBREAD:

1	cup (2 sticks) unsalted butter, at room temperature
1/2	cup finely grated Parmesan cheese
2	cups all-purpose flour
1/2	teaspoon salt

FOR THE TOPPING:

8	fresh figs, quartered
2	tablespoons honey
	A pinch of flaky sea salt
	Fresh thyme leaves, for garnish

Prep Time: 15 minutes
Cook Time: 20 minutes
Total Time: 35 minutes
Servings: 4-6

Preheat your oven to 325°F (165°C) and line a baking sheet with parchment paper. In a large bowl or stand mixer, cream together the butter and Parmesan cheese until smooth. Slowly add in the flour and salt, mixing until a dough forms. Turn out the dough onto a lightly floured surface and knead it gently until it comes together. Roll the dough out to a 1/4 inch thickness and cut out rounds using a 2-inch cookie cutter. Transfer the rounds to the prepared baking sheet and bake for 20 minutes, or until lightly golden.

Allow the shortbreads to cool on the baking sheet for 5 minutes, then transfer them to a wire rack to cool completely. Top each shortbread with a fig quarter, drizzle with honey, sprinkle with sea salt, and garnish with thyme leaves before serving.

Wine Pairing:
The savory, buttery flavors of the Parmesan shortbread and the sweetness of the figs make this appetizer an ideal match for a slightly sweet and aromatic dessert wine like a late-harvest Riesling or a mellow, fruity Port.

Perfectly crisp flatbread adorned with juicy pears, creamy brie, and crunchy walnuts is an elegant yet simple appetizer that delivers a symphony of flavors and textures. Drizzled with a balsamic glaze, this dish is a satisfying start to any meal.

PEAR, BRIE, AND WALNUT FLATBREAD

1	pre-made flatbread or pizza crust
2	tablespoons olive oil
1	large pear, thinly sliced
6 oz	Brie cheese, thinly sliced
1/2	cup walnuts, chopped
2	tablespoons balsamic glaze
1	tablespoon fresh thyme leaves
	Salt and black pepper to taste

Prep Time: 10 minutes
Cook Time: 15 minutes
Total Time: 25 minutes
Servings: 4

Preheat your oven to 425°F (220°C) and place the flatbread on a baking sheet. Drizzle the flatbread with olive oil and arrange the pear slices and Brie cheese evenly on top. Sprinkle the chopped walnuts over the pear and Brie. Season with salt and pepper, and then place in the oven for about 10-15 minutes, or until the cheese is melty and the edges of the flatbread are golden brown.

Remove the flatbread from the oven and let it cool slightly before drizzling with the balsamic glaze and sprinkling with fresh thyme leaves. Cut into slices and serve immediately.

Wine Pairing:
The crisp, juicy pear and creamy Brie make a perfect pairing with a medium-bodied white wine such as a Viognier or a lightly oaked Chardonnay. These wines complement the sweet and savory flavors without overpowering them.

Bite-sized and bursting with flavor, these Sweet Potato Rounds topped with creamy goat cheese and tangy cranberry relish are a vibrant, crowd-pleasing appetizer. Simple to make, yet delightfully gourmet, these are perfect for keeping your date night fancy but fuss-free.

Sweet Potato Rounds with Goat Cheese and Cranberry

2	large sweet potatoes, sliced into 1/2-inch rounds
3	tablespoons olive oil
4 oz	goat cheese, crumbled
1	cup cranberry relish (store-bought or homemade)
	Salt and black pepper, to taste

Prep Time: 15 minutes
Cook Time: 25 minutes
Total Time: 40 minutes
Servings: 6 (approx. 24 rounds)

Preheat your oven to 400 degrees F (200 degrees C) and line a baking sheet with parchment paper. Arrange the sweet potato rounds on the prepared baking sheet. Drizzle with olive oil, then sprinkle with salt and pepper. Toss to coat evenly. Bake the sweet potato rounds in the preheated oven for about 25 minutes, or until they're tender and slightly caramelized around the edges. Flip them halfway through the baking time to ensure even cooking.

Once the sweet potato rounds are cooked, let them cool for a few minutes. Then, top each round with a generous sprinkle of crumbled goat cheese. Place a dollop of cranberry relish on top of the goat cheese. If you like, you can put the rounds back in the oven for a couple of minutes to warm up the toppings.

Serve the sweet potato rounds immediately as a warm appetizer. Enjoy this delightful combination of sweet, tangy, and creamy flavors!

Note: For a twist, try adding a sprinkle of chopped fresh herbs (such as rosemary or thyme) before serving, or drizzle with a balsamic reduction.

Wine Pairing:
A white wine like a Chardonnay or a Viognier tend to have a good balance of fruit and acidity that can stand up to the tang of the goat cheese and the sweetness of the sweet potato and cranberry.

If you prefer red, a light Pinot Noir could also be a great option. Its fruit-forward profile and light tannins can complement the flavors without overwhelming them.

SALAD

This vibrant, refreshing salad features an array of citrus fruits, crisp fennel, and a sweet and tangy honey vinaigrette. The combination of bright citrus, slightly sweet and crunchy fennel, and the honey vinaigrette creates a beautifully balanced and incredibly flavorful dish.

CITRUS AND FENNEL SALAD WITH HONEY VINAIGRETTE

FOR THE SALAD:

1	large fennel bulb, thinly sliced
2	oranges, peeled and segmented
1	grapefruit, peeled and segmented
1	blood orange, peeled and segmented
1/4	red onion, thinly sliced
1/4	cup fresh mint, chopped

FOR THE HONEY VINAIGRETTE:

2	tablespoons honey
2	tablespoons apple cider vinegar
1/4	cup extra-virgin olive oil
	Salt and pepper to taste

Prep Time: 20 minutes
Cook Time: 0 minutes
Total Time: 20 minutes
Servings: 4

In a large salad bowl, combine the thinly sliced fennel, segmented oranges, grapefruit, blood orange, and red onion.

For the vinaigrette, in a small bowl, whisk together the honey, apple cider vinegar, olive oil, salt, and pepper until well combined. Drizzle the vinaigrette over the salad and toss gently to combine. Sprinkle the salad with the chopped fresh mint just before serving.

Wine Pairing:
A well-chilled Sauvignon Blanc would complement this salad beautifully. The wine's citrus notes will echo the flavors in the salad, while its acidity will balance the sweetness of the honey vinaigrette.

This elegantly simple salad delivers on both taste and visual appeal. The slightly bitter frisée lettuce pairs beautifully with the creamy, warm goat cheese, and the tangy vinaigrette ties everything together.

Frisée Salad with Warm Goat Cheese

1	large head frisée lettuce, torn into bite-size pieces
4 oz	goat cheese
1/2	cup panko breadcrumbs
1	egg, beaten
2	tablespoons olive oil
1/2	cup balsamic vinaigrette (your favorite store-bought or homemade)
	Salt and black pepper to taste

Prep Time: 10 minutes
Cook Time: 8 minutes
Total Time: 18 minutes
Servings: 4

Preheat the oven to 375°F (190°C) and line a baking sheet with parchment paper. Slice the goat cheese into four equal rounds. Dip each round into the beaten egg, then coat in panko breadcrumbs. Place the coated goat cheese rounds onto the prepared baking sheet. Bake the goat cheese in the preheated oven for 6-8 minutes, or until the cheese is warm and slightly softened, but not melted.

While the cheese is baking, toss the frisée lettuce with the balsamic vinaigrette. Season with salt and pepper to taste. Divide the dressed lettuce among four plates. Top each salad with a warm goat cheese round. Serve immediately while the goat cheese is still warm.

Wine Pairing:
A Sauvignon Blanc or a crisp, unoaked Chardonnay will beautifully complement the creamy goat cheese and the tangy vinaigrette in this salad. These wines offer the necessary acidity to balance the richness of the cheese and the sweetness of the balsamic dressing.

Fresh, juicy, and slightly charred peaches meet creamy burrata cheese in this summer-inspired salad. It's a symphony of flavors and textures that elevates a simple salad into something memorable.

GRILLED PEACH AND BURRATA SALAD

4	ripe peaches, halved and pitted
2	tablespoons olive oil
8	cups mixed greens
2	balls of burrata cheese
1/4	cup balsamic glaze
1/4	cup chopped fresh basil
	Salt and pepper to taste

Prep Time: 15 minutes
Cook Time: 5 minutes
Total Time: 20 minutes
Servings: 4

Preheat your grill to medium-high heat. Brush the peach halves with olive oil and season with salt and pepper. Place them cut side down on the grill. Grill for about 4-5 minutes, until the peaches are soft and have grill marks. Remove from the grill and let them cool.

Arrange the mixed greens on a platter. Top with the grilled peaches and burrata cheese. Drizzle the salad with balsamic glaze and sprinkle with chopped basil. Serve immediately.

Wine Pairing:
A chilled glass of Prosecco would be a great match for this salad. The wine's light, fruity character complements the sweet grilled peaches, while its bubbles and acidity provide a refreshing contrast to the rich burrata.

Add a smoky twist to your salad course with this Grilled Romaine Salad with Avocado-Lime Dressing. The grilling process brings out a unique flavor in the lettuce that's perfectly balanced by the creamy, tangy dressing.

GRILLED ROMAINE SALAD
WITH AVOCADO-LIME DRESSING

Prep Time: 15 minutes
Cook Time: 5 minutes
Total Time: 20 minutes
Servings: 4

FOR THE SALAD:

2   heads of romaine lettuce, halved lengthwise
2   tablespoons olive oil
1/2   cup cherry tomatoes, halved
1/4   cup feta cheese, crumbled
Salt and pepper to taste

FOR THE AVOCADO-LIME DRESSING:

1   ripe avocado, peeled and pitted
1   lime, juiced
2   tablespoons olive oil
2   tablespoons Greek yogurt
2   tablespoons fresh cilantro leaves
Salt and pepper to taste

Preheat your grill to medium-high heat. Brush the cut sides of the romaine lettuce with olive oil and season with salt and pepper. Place the lettuce halves cut-side down on the grill. Cook for about 2-3 minutes, until slightly charred and wilted.

For the dressing, combine the avocado, lime juice, olive oil, Greek yogurt, salt, pepper, and cilantro leaves in a blender or food processor. Blend until smooth.

Arrange the grilled lettuce on serving plates, cut side up. Drizzle the avocado-lime dressing over the lettuce, then top with halved cherry tomatoes and crumbled feta cheese.

Wine Pairing:
A crisp Chardonnay with notes of green apple and citrus will complement the smoky romaine and tangy dressing in this salad, enhancing the overall dining experience.

Experience a delightful symphony of flavors and textures with the asparagus roasted to perfection, bringing out its unique, earthy flavor, which pairs delightfully with the rich, runny yolk of the poached egg. This elegant salad is topped with a tangy lemon vinaigrette that ties it all together beautifully.

ROASTED ASPARAGUS SALAD WITH POACHED EGG

FOR THE SALAD:

Prep Time: 15 minutes
Cook Time: 15 minutes
Total Time: 30 minutes
Servings: 4

1	pound fresh asparagus, ends trimmed
2	tablespoons olive oil
4	large eggs
1	tablespoon vinegar
4	cups mixed salad greens
1/4	cup Parmesan cheese, shaved
	Salt and pepper to taste

FOR THE LEMON VINAIGRETTE:

1/4	cup fresh lemon juice
1/2	cup olive oil
1	teaspoon Dijon mustard
1	garlic clove, minced
	Salt and pepper to taste

Preheat your oven to 425°F (220°C). Toss the asparagus with olive oil and season with salt and pepper. Arrange in a single layer on a baking sheet. Roast for 15 minutes or until tender and lightly browned.

While the asparagus is roasting, make the vinaigrette. Whisk together lemon juice, olive oil, Dijon mustard, garlic, salt, and pepper. Set aside.

Bring a large pot of water to a simmer and add vinegar. Crack an egg into a small cup, then gently slide it into the water. Repeat with the rest of the eggs. Poach for 4 minutes, then remove with a slotted spoon.

Arrange salad greens on plates. Top with roasted asparagus, a poached egg, and a sprinkle of shaved Parmesan. Drizzle with the lemon vinaigrette. Serve immediately.

Wine Pairing:
Pair this elegant salad with a glass of Sauvignon Blanc. Its crispness and citrus undertones will balance the richness of the poached egg and complement the asparagus and lemon vinaigrette.

This salad is a beautiful combination of sweet roasted squash, peppery arugula, and juicy pomegranate seeds, creating a burst of flavor and color. Dressed in a light lemon vinaigrette, it's a refreshing yet comforting choice.

ROASTED SQUASH AND ARUGULA SALAD
WITH POMEGRANATE

FOR THE SALAD:

Prep Time: 15 minutes
Cook Time: 25 minutes
Total Time: 40 minutes
Servings: 4

1 medium butternut squash, peeled and cubed

2 tablespoons olive oil

5 cups arugula

1 cup pomegranate seeds

1/4 cup feta cheese, crumbled

Salt and pepper to taste

FOR THE LEMON VINAIGRETTE:

1/4 cup extra virgin olive oil

1 lemon, juiced

1 teaspoon Dijon mustard

Salt and pepper to taste

Preheat your oven to 400°F (200°C). Toss the cubed butternut squash with olive oil, salt, and pepper and spread out on a baking sheet. Roast for 20-25 minutes, or until the squash is tender and caramelized.

While the squash is roasting, prepare the vinaigrette by whisking together the olive oil, lemon juice, Dijon mustard, salt, and pepper. Adjust to taste.

In a large bowl, combine the arugula, roasted squash, pomegranate seeds, and feta cheese. Drizzle with the lemon vinaigrette and gently toss to combine. Serve the salad immediately.

Wine Pairing:
A Sauvignon Blanc, with its crisp acidity and citrus notes, complements the peppery arugula and tart pomegranate, while also standing up to the sweet, roasted squash.

This fresh, flavorful, elegant salad showcases the delicate, sweet flavor of seared scallops, paired with a vibrant mix of mixed greens and a citrus vinaigrette.

SEARED SCALLOP SALAD WITH CITRUS VINAIGRETTE

FOR THE SALAD:

12	sea scallops
1	tablespoon olive oil
6	cups mixed greens
1/2	red onion, thinly sliced
1/2	cup cherry tomatoes, halved
	Salt and pepper to taste

FOR THE CITRUS VINAIGRETTE:

1/4	cup fresh orange juice
2	tablespoons fresh lemon juice
1/2	cup olive oil
1	teaspoon honey
	Salt and pepper to taste

Prep Time: 10 minutes
Cook Time: 5 minutes
Total Time: 15 minutes
Servings: 2

Rinse the scallops and pat them dry. Season with salt and pepper. Heat olive oil in a skillet over medium-high heat. Add scallops and sear until golden brown, about 2 minutes per side. Remove from heat.

In a large bowl, combine mixed greens, red onion, and cherry tomatoes. For the vinaigrette, whisk together orange juice, lemon juice, olive oil, and honey in a small bowl. Season with salt and pepper to taste. Drizzle vinaigrette over the salad and toss to combine. Top the salad with the seared scallops and serve immediately.

Wine Pairing:
A Sauvignon Blanc pairs well with this dish, its bright acidity and citrus notes perfectly complementing the seared scallops and citrus vinaigrette.

Experience an elegant and refreshing salad featuring slices of rich, smoky duck breast paired with sweet, juicy oranges. Tossed with mixed greens and a zesty orange vinaigrette, this salad is a perfect balance of flavors and textures.

SMOKED DUCK AND ORANGE SALAD

FOR THE SALAD:

Prep Time: 20 minutes
Cook Time: 0 minutes
Total Time: 20 minutes
Servings: 4

2	smoked duck breasts
3	large oranges
6	cups mixed salad greens
1/2	red onion, thinly sliced
1/2	cup toasted walnut halves
	Salt and pepper to taste

FOR THE ORANGE VINAIGRETTE:

1/4	cup fresh orange juice (from one of the oranges)
1/4	cup extra-virgin olive oil
1	tablespoon Dijon mustard
1	tablespoon honey
	Salt and pepper to taste

Slice the duck breasts thinly. Peel and segment two of the oranges, reserving any juice for the vinaigrette.

For the vinaigrette, in a small bowl, whisk together the orange juice, olive oil, Dijon mustard, honey, salt, and pepper until emulsified.

In a large salad bowl, combine the mixed greens, orange segments, red onion slices, and toasted walnut halves. Drizzle over the vinaigrette and toss until well combined.

Arrange the salad on plates and top with the sliced smoked duck breast. Season with a pinch of salt and pepper, if desired, and serve.

Wine Pairing:
A chilled glass of Gewürztraminer, with its aromatics and slightly sweet profile, will complement the smoky duck and sweet citrus flavors in this salad excellently. The wine's good acidity will balance the richness of the duck and the sweetness of the oranges.

This Thai beef salad strikes a lovely balance between savory, sweet, and spicy, with tender slices of beef, crispy fried shallots, and a zesty lime dressing. It's a taste adventure that is both refreshing and satisfying.

THAI BEEF SALAD WITH CRISPY SHALLOTS

FOR THE SALAD:

Prep Time: 15 minutes
Cook Time: 15 minutes
Total Time: 30 minutes
Servings: 2

1	pound sirloin steak
2	tablespoons vegetable oil
2	large shallots, thinly sliced
6	cups mixed greens
1	cup fresh mint leaves
1	cup fresh cilantro leaves
1	cucumber, thinly sliced
2	scallions, thinly sliced
1/2	cup roasted peanuts, chopped
	Salt and pepper to taste

FOR THE DRESSING:

2	tablespoons fish sauce
2	limes, juiced
1	tablespoon brown sugar
1	small red chili, finely chopped

Season the steak with salt and pepper. Heat a skillet over high heat, add the steak, and sear until desired doneness. Allow the steak to rest for a few minutes, then slice thinly.

Heat the vegetable oil in a small skillet over medium heat. Add the shallots and fry until crispy and golden brown. Drain on paper towels.

In a large bowl, combine mixed greens, mint leaves, cilantro leaves, cucumber, scallions, and peanuts.

For the dressing, whisk together fish sauce, lime juice, brown sugar, and chili in a small bowl. Drizzle dressing over the salad and toss to combine. Top the salad with the sliced steak and crispy shallots. Serve immediately.

Wine Pairing:
Pair this Thai beef salad with a German Riesling. The wine's sweetness will nicely balance the spice in the salad while its acidity will cut through the savory beef.

This refreshing and vibrant salad perfectly encapsulates the essence of summer. The juicy sweetness of the watermelon, the salty creaminess of the feta, and the bright freshness of the mint create a delicious harmony of flavors that's ideal for a light starter or side dish.

WATERMELON, FETA, AND MINT SALAD

4	cups of watermelon, cubed
1	cup of feta cheese, crumbled
1/4	cup of fresh mint leaves, roughly torn
1/2	red onion, thinly sliced
2	tablespoons of olive oil
1	lime, juiced
	Salt and pepper to taste

Prep Time: 15 minutes
Cook Time: 0 minutes
Total Time: 15 minutes
Servings: 4

In a large salad bowl, combine the watermelon, feta, mint leaves, and red onion. In a small bowl, whisk together the olive oil, lime juice, salt, and pepper. Adjust seasoning to taste. Drizzle the dressing over the salad and gently toss to combine.

Chill the salad in the refrigerator for about 15-20 minutes before serving to allow the flavors to meld together. Serve the salad chilled.

Wine Pairing:
A Rosé or a dry Riesling would be a delightful pairing with this salad. These wines have the crisp acidity needed to balance the sweetness of the watermelon and the richness of the feta, while also complementing the freshness of the mint.

SIDE

Indulge in the rich, velvety texture of this Creamy Mascarpone Polenta. Infused with creamy mascarpone cheese, this polenta is the perfect comforting side dish that pairs beautifully with a variety of main courses.

CREAMY MASCARPONE POLENTA

1	cup polenta
4	cups chicken or vegetable broth
1	teaspoon salt
1/2	cup mascarpone cheese
2	tablespoons unsalted butter
1/4	cup Parmesan cheese, grated
	Freshly ground black pepper, to taste
	Fresh parsley, chopped, for garnish

Prep Time: 5 minutes
Cook Time: 20 minutes
Total Time: 25 minutes
Servings: 4

In a large saucepan, bring the broth and salt to a boil. Gradually whisk in the polenta, reduce the heat to low, and cook, stirring often, until the polenta is tender and the mixture is thickened, about 15-20 minutes. Remove the pan from the heat, then stir in the mascarpone cheese, butter, and Parmesan cheese until well combined. Season with black pepper to taste. Transfer the polenta to a serving dish, garnish with chopped fresh parsley, and serve warm.

Wine Pairing:
A medium-bodied white wine such as Vermentino or a lighter red like Pinot Noir would pair beautifully with this creamy dish, as these wines offer a nice balance to the richness of the polenta without overpowering it.

Experience the ultimate balance of texture and flavor with these Crispy Smashed Potatoes. Tossed in garlic and herbs, these potatoes are a delightfully crunchy treat on the outside while staying irresistibly soft on the inside. It's an impressive and easy-to-make side dish that's sure to be a hit.

CRISPY SMASHED POTATOES
WITH GARLIC AND HERBS

1 1/2   pounds baby potatoes
4   tablespoons olive oil
2   cloves garlic, minced
1   teaspoon fresh rosemary, finely chopped
1   teaspoon fresh thyme, finely chopped
          Salt and freshly ground black pepper, to taste
          Fresh parsley, for garnish

Prep Time: 10 minutes
Cook Time: 40 minutes
Total Time: 50 minutes
Servings: 4

Preheat your oven to 450°F (230°C). While the oven is preheating, place the potatoes in a large pot with salted water. Bring to a boil and cook until the potatoes are fork-tender, about 15-20 minutes. Drain the potatoes and let them dry for a few minutes. Transfer the potatoes to a baking sheet. Using the bottom of a glass or a potato masher, gently smash each potato.

In a small bowl, combine the olive oil, minced garlic, rosemary, thyme, salt, and pepper. Brush the potatoes with half of this mixture. Bake the potatoes in the preheated oven for about 15-20 minutes or until crispy and golden brown. Remove from the oven and brush with the remaining garlic and herb mixture. Garnish with fresh parsley before serving.

Wine Pairing:
These crispy potatoes would pair wonderfully with a full-bodied white wine such as a Chardonnay, which can complement the herb and garlic flavors. Alternatively, a light-bodied red wine like a Grenache could also work well with this dish.

These elegant French green beans are sautéed with shallots and topped with toasted almonds for a wonderful crunch. It's a sophisticated side dish that requires only a few ingredients but delivers big on flavor.

FRENCH GREEN BEANS
WITH SHALLOTS AND ALMONDS

1	pound French green beans, ends trimmed
2	tablespoons olive oil
2	shallots, finely chopped
1/3	cup almonds, slivered and toasted
	Salt and freshly ground black pepper to taste

Prep Time: 10 minutes
Cook Time: 10 minutes
Total Time: 20 minutes
Servings: 4

Bring a large pot of salted water to a boil. Add the green beans and blanch for 2 minutes until bright green but still crisp. Drain and immediately plunge into an ice bath to stop the cooking process. Once cooled, drain and pat dry.

In a large skillet over medium heat, heat the olive oil. Add the chopped shallots and sauté until soft and translucent, about 3-4 minutes. Add the green beans to the skillet, season with salt and pepper, and toss well. Sauté for another 2-3 minutes, or until the beans are heated through but still retain a bite. Transfer the green beans to a serving dish and top with the toasted almonds. Serve warm.

Wine Pairing:
The freshness of the green beans, coupled with the nuttiness of the almonds, would pair well with a white Burgundy or a medium-bodied, citrusy Sauvignon Blanc. These wines can complement the flavors without overpowering the dish.

Rich, garlicky, and wonderfully savory, these sautéed mushrooms are cooked in butter until golden brown, then finished with a generous helping of minced garlic. This side dish offers an impressive depth of flavor.

GARLIC BUTTER SAUTÉED MUSHROOMS

1   pound mixed mushrooms (cremini, button, shiitake), cleaned and sliced

3   tablespoons unsalted butter

4   cloves garlic, minced

Salt and freshly ground black pepper to taste

Fresh parsley, chopped, for garnish

Prep Time: 10 minutes
Cook Time: 15 minutes
Total Time: 25 minutes
Servings: 4

Heat a large skillet over medium heat and add the butter. Once melted, add the mushrooms. Sauté the mushrooms until they are nicely browned and all the liquid they release has evaporated, around 8-10 minutes. Add the minced garlic to the pan, stir well, and cook for another minute or two until the garlic is fragrant but not burnt. Season with salt and pepper to taste and garnish with chopped fresh parsley. Serve immediately.

Wine Pairing:
The earthy flavor of mushrooms pairs beautifully with a medium-bodied Pinot Noir. The wine's fruity notes will complement the savory garlic and mushroom flavors, creating a well-rounded taste profile.

Experience a taste sensation with these Herb Butter Roasted Carrots. The natural sweetness of the carrots paired with fragrant herbs and rich, melted butter make for a side dish that's simple to prepare but delivers on flavor.

HERB BUTTER ROASTED CARROTS

1	pound of baby carrots, scrubbed clean
4	tablespoons of unsalted butter, melted
2	teaspoons of fresh rosemary, minced
2	teaspoons of fresh thyme, minced
	Salt and freshly ground black pepper to taste
	Fresh parsley, chopped, for garnish

Prep Time: 10 minutes
Cook Time: 25 minutes
Total Time: 35 minutes
Servings: 4

Preheat your oven to 400°F (200°C) and line a baking sheet with parchment paper. In a large mixing bowl, combine the melted butter, minced rosemary, and thyme. Add the baby carrots to the bowl and toss until they're well coated in the herb butter mixture. Arrange the carrots on the prepared baking sheet in a single layer. Sprinkle with salt and pepper to taste. Roast the carrots in the preheated oven for 20-25 minutes, or until they're tender and lightly caramelized. Remove from the oven and garnish with freshly chopped parsley before serving.

Wine Pairing:
A vibrant, citrusy Sauvignon Blanc would work wonderfully with this dish. The wine's acidity and brightness will balance out the richness of the butter and contrast nicely with the sweet, earthy carrots.

This Honey Sriracha Roasted Cauliflower dish offers a delightful balance of sweet and spicy, all while being crispy, tender, and downright delicious. Perfect for those who crave a bit of heat on their plates.

HONEY SRIRACHA ROASTED CAULIFLOWER

1	head of cauliflower, cut into florets
3	tablespoons of olive oil
3	tablespoons of honey
2	tablespoons of Sriracha sauce
1	tablespoon of soy sauce
1	tablespoon of lime juice
2	cloves of garlic, minced
2	tablespoons of fresh cilantro, chopped, for garnish
	Salt to taste

Prep Time: 10 minutes
Cook Time: 30 minutes
Total Time: 40 minutes
Servings: 4

Preheat your oven to 425°F (220°C) and line a baking sheet with parchment paper. In a large bowl, combine cauliflower florets, olive oil, and salt. Toss to ensure each piece is coated. Spread the cauliflower in a single layer on the prepared baking sheet. Roast the cauliflower in the preheated oven for about 20 minutes, or until it starts to brown and become tender.

While the cauliflower roasts, in a small bowl, mix together the honey, Sriracha sauce, soy sauce, lime juice, and minced garlic. Remove the cauliflower from the oven and drizzle the honey Sriracha mixture over it. Toss to ensure all pieces are coated. Return the baking sheet to the oven and roast for another 5-10 minutes, or until the cauliflower is caramelized and crispy. Garnish with chopped cilantro before serving.

Wine Pairing:
A semi-dry Riesling would pair beautifully with this dish. The wine's light sweetness can cool the palate from the heat of the Sriracha, and its crisp acidity can cut through the rich flavors. Its notes of citrus and stone fruit also compliment the cauliflower and honey in the dish.

This Roasted Red Pepper and Feta Stuffed Tomatoes dish makes a visually striking and deliciously savory side dish. Each bite offers a burst of Mediterranean flavors that's sure to impress.

ROASTED RED PEPPER
AND FETA STUFFED TOMATOES

4	large tomatoes
1	cup of roasted red peppers, finely chopped
3/4	cup of feta cheese, crumbled
1/4	cup of fresh basil leaves, chopped
2	cloves of garlic, minced
2	tablespoons of olive oil
1/4	cup of bread crumbs
2	tablespoons of Parmesan cheese, grated
	Salt and pepper to taste

Prep Time: 15 minutes
Cook Time: 25 minutes
Total Time: 40 minutes
Servings: 4

Preheat your oven to 375°F (190°C). Slice off the tops of the tomatoes and scoop out the insides, leaving a thick shell. Discard the seeds and chop the remaining pulp. In a bowl, combine the chopped tomato pulp, roasted red peppers, feta cheese, basil, garlic, olive oil, salt, and pepper. Fill the tomato shells with the mixture and place them in a baking dish. Top each tomato with bread crumbs and grated Parmesan. Bake in the preheated oven for about 20-25 minutes, or until the tomatoes are tender and the tops are golden.

Wine Pairing:
A chilled glass of Sauvignon Blanc would pair wonderfully with this dish. The wine's high acidity and herbaceous notes will complement the tangy feta and sweet roasted peppers, while also balancing the richness of the cheese.

This Sautéed Broccolini with Garlic and Lemon recipe delivers a perfect side dish that's quick, easy, and loaded with fresh and tangy flavors. The slight crunch of the broccolini coupled with the zest of the lemon and the bite of the garlic make it an ideal complement to any main course.

SAUTÉED BROCCOLINI WITH GARLIC AND LEMON

2	bunches of broccolini, ends trimmed
2	tablespoons of olive oil
4	cloves of garlic, thinly sliced
1	lemon, zest and juice
	Salt and pepper to taste
	Chili flakes (optional)

Prep Time: 10 minutes
Cook Time: 7 minutes
Total Time: 17 minutes
Servings: 4

In a large frying pan, heat the olive oil over medium heat. Add the garlic and sauté until it becomes fragrant and lightly golden, about 1 minute. Add the broccolini to the pan, season with salt, pepper, and chili flakes (if using), then cover and cook for about 5 minutes, or until it's tender-crisp. Stir occasionally. Remove the cover and stir in the lemon zest and juice. Continue to cook for another 2 minutes. Serve the broccolini warm, ensuring to spoon some of the garlic and pan juices over top before serving.

Wine Pairing:
A crisp and vibrant white wine, such as a Vermentino or a Chablis, would pair wonderfully with this dish. The wine's acidity and citrus notes will harmonize with the lemon and balance out the green and garlicky flavors of the broccolini.

These Sweet and Spicy Glazed Brussels Sprouts are caramelized to perfection with a sticky sweet and spicy glaze. The heat from the chili and the sweetness from the honey make these Brussels sprouts a memorable side dish, sure to win over even the pickiest eaters.

SWEET AND SPICY GLAZED BRUSSELS SPROUTS

1 1/2	pounds of Brussels sprouts, ends trimmed and halved
2	tablespoons of olive oil
2	tablespoons of honey
1	tablespoon of hot sauce (adjust to taste)
1	tablespoon of apple cider vinegar
	Salt and pepper to taste

Prep Time: 10 minutes
Cook Time: 25 minutes
Total Time: 35 minutes
Servings: 4

Preheat your oven to 425°F (220°C). Toss Brussels sprouts with olive oil, salt, and pepper in a large bowl. Ensure they're all evenly coated. Spread Brussels sprouts in a single layer on a baking sheet. Roast in the preheated oven for about 20 minutes, or until the sprouts are tender and edges are crispy.

While the sprouts are roasting, mix together the honey, hot sauce, and apple cider vinegar in a small bowl. Remove the Brussels sprouts from the oven and drizzle the glaze over them. Toss well to coat. Return to the oven for another 5 minutes, or until the glaze is sticky and sprouts are well caramelized. Serve hot, ideally straight from the oven.

Wine Pairing:
Pair these Brussels sprouts with an off-dry Riesling. The wine's inherent sweetness will balance the spiciness and complement the honey in the glaze. Plus, the zesty acidity of the Riesling will provide a nice contrast to the earthy Brussels sprouts.

This Sweet Potato Gratin with Gruyère is a luxurious twist on the classic potato gratin. Thinly sliced sweet potatoes are layered with a rich cream and fragrant thyme, then topped with nutty Gruyère cheese.

SWEET POTATO GRATIN WITH GRUYÈRE

2	pounds of sweet potatoes, peeled and thinly sliced
1	cup of heavy cream
1/2	cup of whole milk
2	cloves of garlic, minced
1	teaspoon of fresh thyme leaves, plus extra for garnish
1.5	cups of Gruyère cheese, grated
	Salt and freshly ground black pepper to taste

Prep Time: 20 minutes
Cook Time: 60 minutes
Total Time: 80 minutes
Servings: 6

Preheat your oven to 375°F (190°C) and lightly grease a baking dish. In a saucepan over medium heat, combine the heavy cream, milk, garlic, thyme, salt, and pepper. Bring to a simmer. Arrange half of the sweet potato slices in the prepared baking dish, overlapping slightly. Pour half of the cream mixture over the potatoes, then sprinkle half of the Gruyère on top. Repeat with the remaining potatoes, cream mixture, and Gruyère. Cover the dish with aluminum foil and bake for 30 minutes. Remove the foil and bake for another 20-30 minutes, or until the top is golden and bubbly and the potatoes are tender. Let the gratin rest for 10 minutes before serving, garnishing with extra thyme leaves if desired.

Wine Pairing:
Try pairing this dish with a full-bodied, oaked Chardonnay. The wine's buttery notes will harmonize with the creaminess of the gratin, while its bright acidity will cut through the richness of the cheese and cream.

MAIN

Coq au Vin is a classic French stew in which chicken is braised slowly in red wine and a little brandy to yield a supremely rich sauce filled with tender meat, mushrooms, onions, and crispy bits of bacon. Our version highlights the nuanced flavors of a French Pinot Noir, providing an indulgent main course.

Coq au Vin

6	bone-in, skin-on chicken thighs	
4 oz	bacon, cut into small pieces	
1	large onion, chopped	
2	carrots, chopped	
3	cloves of garlic, minced	
2	cups French Pinot Noir	
1/4	cup brandy	
2	cups chicken broth	
2	tablespoons tomato paste	
4	sprigs fresh thyme	
2	sprigs fresh rosemary	
1	bay leaf	
2	cups pearl onions, peeled	
2	cups button mushrooms, quartered	
2	tablespoons unsalted butter	
2	tablespoons all-purpose flour	
	Salt and freshly ground black pepper, to taste	

Prep Time: 20 minutes
Cook Time: 1 hour, 20 minutes
Total Time: 1 hour, 40 minutes
Servings: 4-6

Season the chicken thighs with salt and pepper. In a large dutch oven or heavy pot, cook the bacon over medium heat until crisp. Remove the bacon, leaving the fat in the pot. In the same pot, brown the chicken thighs on both sides, remove and set aside. Add the chopped onions, carrots, and garlic. Cook until softened, about 5 minutes. Add the wine, brandy, chicken broth, and tomato paste to the pot. Stir well, scraping the bottom of the pot to release any browned bits. Add the thyme, rosemary, and bay leaf, then return the chicken and bacon to the pot. Bring to a simmer and cook, covered, for about 1 hour.

In a separate pan, melt the butter over medium heat. Add the pearl onions and mushrooms, cooking until golden brown. Sprinkle the flour over the onions and mushrooms, stirring well to coat. Cook for another 2 minutes, then add this mixture to the pot with the chicken. Cook for another 10 minutes, until the sauce is thickened. Remove the bay leaf, and any thyme and rosemary stems. Taste and adjust seasoning with more salt and pepper if needed. Serve the Coq au Vin hot, garnished with fresh parsley.

Wine Pairing:
Pair with the French Pinot Noir used for cooking. The wine's bright fruit character and earthy undertones work wonderfully with the dish's hearty and rich profile.

For an unforgettable romantic meal, serve this Espresso Rubbed Filet Mignon. The bold, slightly bitter espresso crust is balanced beautifully by the inherent sweetness of the high-quality beef and a hint of brown sugar. Paired with a Cabernet Sauvignon, it's a main course that will impress without question.

ESPRESSO RUBBED FILET MIGNON

4	filet mignon steaks (about 1.5 inches thick)
2	tablespoons finely ground espresso
1	tablespoon brown sugar
1	teaspoon coarse sea salt
1	teaspoon freshly ground black pepper
2	tablespoons olive oil

Prep Time: 10 minutes
Cook Time: 10 minutes
Total Time: 20 minutes
Servings: 4

Preheat your grill or stovetop grill pan to high heat. In a small bowl, mix together the finely ground espresso, brown sugar, sea salt, and black pepper to make the rub. Pat the filet mignon steaks dry with a paper towel. Rub each steak all over with the olive oil, then coat each steak with the espresso rub, pressing it into the meat. Grill the steaks for about 5 minutes per side for medium-rare, or until it reaches your desired level of doneness. Remove the steaks from the grill and let them rest for 5 minutes before serving. This allows the juices to redistribute throughout the steak.

Wine Pairing:
Serve this Espresso Rubbed Filet Mignon with a robust Cabernet Sauvignon. The wine's strong tannins are smoothed out by the fattiness of the filet mignon, while its dark fruit flavors are the perfect foil for the steak's bitter-sweet espresso crust. Choose a Cabernet from a region known for producing full-bodied examples, like Napa Valley or Bordeaux's Left Bank.

Grilled Swordfish Steaks topped with a tangy Olive Relish make for an elegant and flavorful main course. The hearty swordfish holds up well to the grill, and the olive relish adds a Mediterranean flair. Paired with a glass of crisp Vermentino, this dish is reminiscent of a seaside dinner in Italy.

GRILLED SWORDFISH STEAKS WITH OLIVE RELISH

4	swordfish steaks (about 6 ounces each)
1	cup mixed olives, pitted and chopped
1	small red onion, finely chopped
2	tablespoons capers, rinsed and chopped
1	lemon, zest and juice
1/4	cup extra virgin olive oil, plus extra for brushing
	Salt and freshly ground black pepper
	Fresh parsley, chopped, for garnish

Prep Time: 15 minutes
Cook Time: 8 minutes
Total Time: 23 minutes
Servings: 4

Preheat the grill on medium-high heat. To prepare the olive relish, mix together the chopped olives, red onion, capers, lemon zest and juice, and olive oil in a bowl. Season with salt and pepper to taste, then set aside. Brush the swordfish steaks lightly with olive oil, and season with salt and pepper. Place the steaks on the hot grill and cook for about 3-4 minutes per side, until the fish is opaque and flakes easily with a fork. Remove the swordfish steaks from the grill and let them rest for a couple of minutes. To serve, top each steak with a generous spoonful of the olive relish and garnish with chopped parsley.

Wine Pairing:
This dish pairs beautifully with a glass of Vermentino. This white wine, well-known in Italy's coastal regions, brings a crisp acidity and notes of citrus that complement the robust flavors of the swordfish and the tanginess of the olive relish.

Lobster Thermidor is a classic French dish that exudes elegance and decadence. Succulent lobster meat is sautéed with a creamy white wine sauce, placed back in the shell, topped with Gruyère cheese, and then broiled to perfection. This rich and luxurious dish pairs brilliantly with a glass of crisp, minerally Chablis.

LOBSTER THERMIDOR

2	live lobsters, each about 1-1.5 pounds
4	tablespoons unsalted butter
1	small onion, finely chopped
1	cup dry white wine
1	cup heavy cream
2	tablespoons all-purpose flour
2	egg yolks
1	teaspoon Dijon mustard
1	cup Gruyère cheese, grated
	Salt and freshly ground black pepper
	Fresh parsley, chopped, for garnish

Prep Time: 20 minutes
Cook Time: 30 minutes
Total Time: 50 minutes
Servings: 2

Preheat your broiler. Bring a large pot of salted water to a boil. Add the lobsters and cook for about 8-10 minutes. Remove the lobsters and let them cool. Once cool, cut the lobsters in half lengthwise. Remove the meat from the claws and tail, but leave the shell intact. Cut the lobster meat into bite-size pieces.

In a large skillet over medium heat, melt 2 tablespoons of butter. Add the onion and sauté until translucent, about 5 minutes. Stir in the flour until well blended with the onions and butter. Add the white wine to the pan, and cook until the mixture has reduced by half.

In a bowl, whisk together the heavy cream and egg yolks. Slowly add this mixture to the pan, stirring constantly until the sauce thickens. Stir in the Dijon mustard and season with salt and pepper. Add the lobster meat to the pan and stir until it's well coated with the sauce. Spoon the lobster mixture back into the lobster shells and sprinkle the Gruyère cheese on top. Place the lobster halves on a baking sheet and broil until the cheese is bubbly and golden, about 3-5 minutes. Garnish with fresh parsley before serving.

Wine Pairing:
A Chablis, with its bright acidity and rich, full-bodied character, works perfectly with this dish. The wine's minerality and crisp finish balance out the creaminess of the sauce and highlight the delicate sweetness of the lobster.

This Moroccan-spiced rack of lamb will take your taste buds on a journey to North Africa. A robust mix of spices pairs beautifully with the juicy, succulent lamb, while the light char from the grill adds a smoky complexity. Enjoy this aromatic, flavorful dish with a glass of fruit-forward, spicy Red Zinfandel for a truly unforgettable dining experience.

MOROCCAN-SPICED RACK OF LAMB

2	racks of lamb, about 1.5 pounds each
2	tablespoons olive oil
2	cloves garlic, minced
1	tablespoon ground cumin
1	tablespoon ground coriander
1	teaspoon ground cinnamon
1	teaspoon ground turmeric
1/2	teaspoon cayenne pepper
	Salt and freshly ground black pepper
	Fresh mint, for garnish

Prep Time: 40 minutes
Cook Time: 20 minutes
Total Time: 1 hour
Servings: 4

Preheat your grill on high heat. In a small bowl, combine the olive oil, minced garlic, cumin, coriander, cinnamon, turmeric, cayenne pepper, salt, and black pepper. Rub this spice mixture all over the lamb racks, making sure to coat all sides. Let the lamb marinate for at least 30 minutes, or up to 24 hours in the refrigerator for more flavor. Grill the lamb racks over high heat, bone side down first, for about 7-10 minutes. Then flip and grill for another 7-10 minutes for medium-rare, or until the internal temperature reaches 135°F. Remove the lamb from the grill and let it rest for 10 minutes before cutting into individual chops. Garnish with fresh mint and serve immediately.

Wine Pairing:
A Red Zinfandel, known for its bold, fruity character and spicy undertones, will complement the Moroccan spices in the lamb beautifully. The wine's medium tannins and acidity can hold up to the richness of the lamb, while its berry flavors will complement the smoky, spiced meat.

This classic Italian dish, Osso Buco, is a hearty meal that combines tender veal shanks with a rich, savory tomato and vegetable sauce. The marrow in the bone adds an unmatched depth of flavor that makes this dish stand out. Paired with a Nebbiolo, whose high tannins, acidity, and full body stand up to the robust flavors of the Osso Buco, you've got a meal worthy of a special occasion.

OSSO BUCO

4	veal shanks, about 2 inches thick
1/2	cup all-purpose flour
1/4	cup olive oil
1	onion, chopped
1	carrot, chopped
1	celery stalk, chopped
4	cloves garlic, minced
1	cup Nebbiolo wine
1	can (28 ounces) crushed tomatoes
1	cup chicken stock
1	teaspoon fresh thyme leaves
2	bay leaves
	Salt and freshly ground black pepper
	Gremolata (zest of 1 lemon, 2 cloves garlic minced, and 2 tablespoons chopped fresh parsley)

Prep Time: 30 minutes
Cook Time: 2 hours 30 minutes
Total Time: 3 hours
Servings: 4

Season the veal shanks with salt and pepper, then dredge them in flour, shaking off the excess. Heat the olive oil in a large Dutch oven over medium-high heat. Add the veal shanks and brown on all sides. Remove the shanks and set them aside. In the same pot, add the onion, carrot, celery, and garlic. Cook until the vegetables are softened and lightly browned. Pour in the Nebbiolo wine, scraping the bottom of the pot to lift up any browned bits. Bring to a simmer and let it reduce by half. Add the crushed tomatoes, chicken stock, thyme, and bay leaves to the pot. Return the veal shanks to the pot, nestling them into the liquid. Cover the pot and reduce the heat to low. Simmer for about 2 hours, until the meat is tender and falling off the bone. Prepare the gremolata by combining the lemon zest, minced garlic, and chopped parsley. Serve the Osso Buco hot, sprinkled with the gremolata.

Wine Pairing:
A Nebbiolo, with its high tannins and acidity, is the perfect pairing for this rich and hearty Osso Buco. The wine's full body will complement the robust flavors of the veal and tomato-based sauce, while the earthy notes in the wine will echo the savory elements of the dish.

This indulgent pasta dish showcases the depth and earthiness of wild mushrooms in a hearty ragu. The wide, ribbon-like pappardelle is perfect for capturing the rich sauce, making every bite a delight. Paired with a Chianti Classico, which balances the earthy mushrooms with its fruity and spicy notes, this meal creates a dining experience perfect for your 'Date Night Decadence'.

PAPPARDELLE PASTA WITH WILD MUSHROOM RAGU

1	pound pappardelle pasta
2	tbsp olive oil
1	onion, finely chopped
2	cloves of garlic, minced
1	pound assorted wild mushrooms (like porcini, oyster, and chanterelles), cleaned and sliced
1	cup Chianti Classico
14.5oz	can crushed tomatoes
1	tsp dried thyme
1	tsp dried rosemary
1/2	cup, Parmesan cheese, grated
	Salt and pepper, to taste
	Fresh parsley, chopped, for garnish

Prep Time: 15 minutes
Cook Time: 45 minutes
Total Time: 1 hour
Servings: 4

Heat olive oil in a large skillet over medium heat. Add onion and cook until soft and translucent. Add garlic and cook for another minute. Add the wild mushrooms to the skillet. Cook until they release their liquid and start to brown. Pour in the Chianti Classico, allowing it to simmer and reduce by half. Add the crushed tomatoes, thyme, rosemary, salt, and pepper. Lower the heat and let the sauce simmer for about 30 minutes, until it thickens into a rich ragu.

While the sauce is simmering, cook the pappardelle according to package instructions until al dente. Drain the pasta and toss it with the mushroom ragu, ensuring the pasta is well coated. Divide the pasta among four plates, top with grated Parmesan cheese, and garnish with fresh parsley.

Wine Pairing:
The earthiness of the mushrooms and the richness of the ragu pair beautifully with a Chianti Classico. The wine's bright acidity and firm tannins balance the hearty dish while its fruit-forward notes bring a touch of freshness to this decadent meal.

The Pistachio Crusted Seared Ahi Tuna is an elegant dish that is surprisingly simple to prepare. The richness of the tuna pairs beautifully with the crunch of the pistachio crust, while the searing locks in the flavors. This dish is the epitome of luxury, especially when served alongside a glass of Pinot Noir, whose light-bodied nature and fruit forward character complement the tuna perfectly.

PISTACHIO CRUSTED SEARED AHI TUNA

Prep Time: 10 minutes
Cook Time: 10 minutes
Total Time: 20 minutes
Servings: 4

FOR THE TUNA:

4	Ahi tuna steaks (about 6 ounces each)
1	cup pistachios, shelled
1	lemon, zested
2	tablespoons olive oil
	Salt and pepper, to taste

FOR THE SAUCE:

1	lemon, juiced
1/4	cup soy sauce
1	tablespoon honey
1	tablespoon fresh ginger, grated
1	clove garlic, minced

Preheat your oven to 400°F (200°C). In a food processor, combine the pistachios and lemon zest. Process until the pistachios are finely chopped but not pasty. Season the tuna steaks with salt and pepper, then press each side into the pistachio mixture to form a crust. Heat the olive oil in a large, oven-safe skillet over medium-high heat. Add the tuna steaks and sear for about 1 minute on each side. Transfer the skillet to the preheated oven and cook for 4-5 minutes, or until the tuna is cooked to your liking.

While the tuna is cooking, prepare the sauce. Combine the lemon juice, soy sauce, honey, ginger, and garlic in a small saucepan over medium heat. Bring to a simmer and cook for about 5 minutes, until the sauce has thickened slightly. Once the tuna is done, serve it with the sauce drizzled on top.

Wine Pairing:
This dish pairs wonderfully with a Pinot Noir. The wine's acidity and light body are a great match for the richness of the tuna, while its fruit-forward profile enhances the nuttiness of the pistachios.

The tenderloin is filled with a savory stuffing and served with a luscious port wine reduction, making it an unforgettable centerpiece to any romantic meal.

STUFFED PORK TENDERLOIN
WITH PORT WINE REDUCTION

FOR THE PORK TENDERLOIN:

2	pork tenderloins (about 1 lb each)
1	cup of fresh spinach, chopped
1/2	cup dried cranberries
1/2	cup goat cheese
	Salt and pepper, to taste

FOR THE PORT WINE REDUCTION:

1	cup Port wine
1	cup beef broth
1	sprig fresh rosemary
2	tablespoons butter

Prep Time: 20 minutes
Cook Time: 30 minutes
Total Time: 50 minutes
Servings: 4

Preheat your oven to 375°F (190°C). Slice the pork tenderloins lengthwise, making sure not to cut all the way through. Open them up like a book and pound to an even thickness. Sprinkle the inside of each tenderloin with salt and pepper. Layer with spinach, cranberries, and goat cheese. Roll up each tenderloin, tucking in the stuffing, and secure with kitchen twine. Season the outside of the tenderloins with salt and pepper, then place in a roasting pan. Roast in the preheated oven for 25-30 minutes, or until a thermometer inserted into the thickest part of the tenderloin reads 145°F (63°C).

While the tenderloins are roasting, prepare the Port wine reduction. In a saucepan, combine the Port wine, beef broth, and rosemary. Simmer over medium heat until reduced by half, about 15-20 minutes. Remove from heat and whisk in the butter. Once the tenderloins are done, let them rest for 5 minutes before slicing. Serve with the Port wine reduction drizzled on top.

Wine Pairing:
A full-bodied Portuguese Douro makes an excellent match for this dish. Its rich, dark fruit flavors and sturdy structure pair wonderfully with the tender, savory pork and sweet Port wine reduction.

This Veal Scallopini recipe is perfect for a luxurious and romantic night in. Tender veal cutlets are lightly breaded and cooked to perfection before being served with a velvety lemon-butter sauce. Paired with a refreshing Soave wine, this dish is truly an elegant experience.

VEAL SCALLOPINI

8	veal cutlets (about 1.5 lbs)
1/2	cup all-purpose flour
4	tablespoons olive oil
2	cloves garlic, minced
1/2	cup dry white wine
1	lemon, juiced
4	tablespoons unsalted butter
1/4	cup fresh parsley, chopped
	Salt and pepper, to taste
	Lemon slices, for garnish

Prep Time: 10 minutes
Cook Time: 20 minutes
Total Time: 30 minutes
Servings: 4

Season the veal cutlets with salt and pepper, then dredge in the flour, shaking off any excess. Heat 2 tablespoons of olive oil in a large skillet over medium-high heat. Add half of the veal cutlets and cook until golden, about 2-3 minutes per side. Remove from the skillet and keep warm. Repeat with the remaining olive oil and veal cutlets. In the same skillet, add the minced garlic and cook until fragrant, about 1 minute. Add the white wine, scraping the bottom of the skillet to loosen any browned bits. Stir in the lemon juice, then reduce heat to low and whisk in the butter one tablespoon at a time until the sauce is smooth and emulsified. Return the veal to the skillet and cook for 1-2 minutes, spooning the sauce over the veal. Sprinkle with chopped parsley and garnish with lemon slices just before serving.

Wine Pairing:
A crisp Soave wine from Italy, known for its light body and notes of citrus and green apple, makes a delightful complement to this dish. Its bright acidity cuts through the rich, buttery sauce, while the light fruit notes enhance the lemony tang. Enjoy!

DESSERT

Our Baked Alaska brings together a moist chocolate sponge cake, smooth ice cream, and a light-as-air meringue topping, all beautifully browned for a striking finish. Paired with a glass of bubbly champagne, it's the perfect sweet ending to a decadent dinner.

BAKED ALASKA

FOR THE CAKE:

3/4	cup all-purpose flour
1/4	cup unsweetened cocoa powder
1	teaspoon baking powder
4	large eggs, room temperature
3/4	cup granulated sugar
	Pinch of salt

FOR THE ASSEMBLY:

1	quart of your favorite ice cream
6	egg whites
1/2	teaspoon cream of tartar
1/2	cup granulated sugar

Prep Time: 20 minutes
Cook Time: 30 minutes
Freeze Time: 2 hours
Total Time: 2 hours, 50 minutes
Servings: 8

Preheat oven to 350°F (175°C). Line a 9-inch round cake pan with parchment paper. In a medium bowl, combine flour, cocoa powder, baking powder, and salt. Set aside. In a large bowl, beat the eggs until frothy. Gradually add sugar and continue beating until the mixture is thick and lemon-colored. Gradually fold in the flour mixture until just combined. Pour the batter into the prepared pan and smooth the top. Bake for 20-25 minutes or until a toothpick inserted into the center comes out clean. Allow to cool completely. Once the cake has cooled, spread the ice cream evenly over the top. Place the cake in the freezer for at least 2 hours, or until the ice cream is firm. Preheat your oven to 500°F (260°C). In a large bowl, beat the egg whites and cream of tartar until soft peaks form. Gradually add sugar, continuing to beat until the meringue is stiff and glossy. Remove the cake from the freezer. Quickly spread the meringue over the ice cream and cake, making sure to seal the edges. Return to the oven and bake for 2-3 minutes, or until the meringue is lightly browned. Serve immediately. Remember, the inside will be very cold while the meringue is hot!

Wine Pairing:
To accompany this dessert, opt for a dry Champagne. Its effervescence will cut through the dessert's richness, while the citrus notes will complement the sweet meringue and ice cream. Enjoy.

Our Crème Brûlée is an irresistible combination of rich, creamy custard and a caramelized sugar crust. This French classic is guaranteed to impress with its luxurious texture and delicate vanilla flavor. Paired with a glass of Sauternes, the dessert becomes an exquisite sweet symphony of tastes and sensations.

Crème Brûlée

2	cups heavy cream
1	vanilla bean, split and seeds scraped out
4	large egg yolks
1/2	cup granulated sugar, plus extra for the caramelized tops
	Hot water, for the water bath

Prep Time: 20 minutes
Cook Time: 45 minutes
Chill Time: 2 hours
Total Time: 3 hours, 5 minutes
Servings: 4

Preheat oven to 325°F (165°C) and position a rack in the center. In a medium saucepan, heat the cream, vanilla bean, and its seeds over medium heat until it begins to simmer. Remove from heat and let steep for 15 minutes.

In a large bowl, beat the egg yolks and sugar until well blended and it starts to lighten in color. Gradually add the cream mixture to the egg yolks, stirring continually. Strain the mixture through a fine sieve into a large pitcher or bowl. Discard the vanilla bean. Pour the custard into four 6-ounce ramekins. Place the ramekins in a baking dish and fill the dish with enough hot water to come halfway up the sides of the ramekins. Bake for 40 to 45 minutes, until the custard is set but still a bit wobbly in the center. Remove from the water bath and let cool to room temperature. Refrigerate for at least 2 hours, or up to 3 days. Before serving, sprinkle each custard with about a teaspoon of sugar. Using a torch, melt the sugar to form a crispy top. If you don't have a torch, you can broil the custards in the oven for a couple of minutes until the sugar melts.

Wine Pairing:
A glass of Sauternes will pair beautifully with this Crème Brûlée. This sweet wine from the Bordeaux region of France will enhance the creamy custard and caramelized sugar, making for a truly divine dessert experience.

Our Dark Chocolate Soufflé is a dessert that never fails to impress. The decadent, airy treat bakes to perfection, with a soft center and a delightful, crusty top. This dessert is a sophisticated ending to a romantic meal, treating the palate to a mix of sweet and slightly bitter flavors.

DARK CHOCOLATE SOUFFLÉ

1/3   cup granulated sugar, plus extra for dusting
5 oz bittersweet chocolate, finely chopped
1   teaspoon pure vanilla extract
3   large egg yolks, at room temperature
6   large egg whites, at room temperature
1/2   teaspoon cream of tartar
       Confectioners' sugar, for dusting

Prep Time: 20 minutes
Cook Time: 25 minutes
Total Time: 45 minutes
Servings: 2-3

Preheat the oven to 400°F (200°C). Lightly butter a 6-cup soufflé dish and dust it with granulated sugar. Melt the chocolate in a heatproof bowl set over a pan of simmering water. Remove from the heat and stir in the vanilla extract. Then stir in the egg yolks one at a time, beating well after each addition. In a large bowl, beat the egg whites with the cream of tartar until soft peaks form. Gradually beat in the remaining granulated sugar until stiff peaks form. Stir about 1/4 of the beaten egg whites into the chocolate mixture to lighten it. Then fold in the remaining egg whites, taking care not to deflate the mixture. Spoon the mixture into the prepared soufflé dish and smooth the top. Bake until the soufflé has puffed and the top is firm and crusty, about 25 minutes. Dust the top with confectioners' sugar and serve immediately.

Wine Pairing:
Pair this Dark Chocolate Soufflé with a glass of Banyuls. This French dessert wine is known for its rich, sweet flavors, which perfectly balance the bittersweet quality of the dark chocolate, creating a harmonious taste experience.

Our New York Cheesecake recipe is a classic dessert that's rich, creamy, and perfectly smooth. The dense, yet velvety cream cheese filling contrasts beautifully with the crunchy graham cracker crust, making every bite heavenly.

NEW YORK CHEESECAKE

FOR THE CRUST:

1 1/2	cups graham cracker crumbs
1/4	cup granulated sugar
1/2	cup unsalted butter, melted

Prep Time: 20 minutes
Cook Time: 1 hour
Cool Time: 6 hours
Total Time: 7 hours, 20 minutes
Servings: 12

FOR THE FILLING:

4	(8-ounce) packages cream cheese, at room temperature
1 1/2	cups granulated sugar
3/4	cup milk
4	large eggs
1	cup sour cream
1	tablespoon vanilla extract
1/4	cup all-purpose flour

Preheat your oven to 325°F (165°C) and lightly grease a 9-inch springform pan. In a medium bowl, mix graham cracker crumbs with sugar, then blend in melted butter. Press the mixture into the bottom of the springform pan. In a large bowl, mix cream cheese with sugar until smooth. Blend in milk, then mix in the eggs one at a time, mixing just enough to incorporate. Mix in sour cream, vanilla, and flour until smooth. Pour the filling over the prepared crust. Bake in preheated oven for 1 hour. Turn the oven off, and let the cheesecake cool in the oven with the door slightly ajar for 5 to 6 hours; this prevents cracking. Chill in the refrigerator until serving.

Wine Pairing:
This creamy New York Cheesecake is perfectly complemented by a glass of Sauternes. The sweetness of this dessert wine matches the richness of the cheesecake, while its high acidity balances the dense, creamy texture, making every bite and sip an exquisite experience.

Light as air, Pavlova with Fresh Berries is an elegant dessert that melts in your mouth. The crisp meringue shell contrasts with the soft, marshmallowy interior, and the tart, juicy berries cut through the sweetness beautifully.

PAVLOVA WITH FRESH BERRIES

FOR THE PAVLOVA:

6	large egg whites, at room temperature
1 1/2	cups granulated sugar
1	teaspoon white vinegar
1	teaspoon cornstarch
1	teaspoon pure vanilla extract

FOR THE TOPPING:

1	cup heavy cream
1	tablespoon powdered sugar
1	teaspoon pure vanilla extract
2	cups mixed fresh berries (such as strawberries, raspberries, and blueberries)

Prep Time: 20 minutes
Cook Time: 1 hour
Cool Time: 2 hours
Total Time: 3 hours, 20 minutes
Servings: 8

Preheat your oven to 300°F (150°C). Draw a 9-inch circle on a sheet of parchment paper and place it on a baking sheet. Beat egg whites in a large bowl until stiff peaks form. Gradually add sugar, one tablespoon at a time, beating well after each addition. Beat until thick and glossy. Gently fold in the vinegar, cornstarch, and vanilla extract. Mound the mixture in the center of the circle on the parchment paper. Smooth the edges, making sure the edges of the meringue are slightly higher than the center. This will make a well for the cream and fruit. Bake for 1 hour. Turn off the oven and let the pavlova cool completely inside the oven. Just before serving, whip the cream with powdered sugar and vanilla until soft peaks form. Spoon into the well of the pavlova. Top with fresh berries and serve immediately.

Wine Pairing:
A glass of Prosecco, with its light, fizzy nature and notes of green apple, honeydew, and cream, is the perfect pairing for this Pavlova. The bubbles and acidity of the Prosecco cut through the sweetness of the dessert and echo the freshness of the berries, creating a harmonious blend of flavors..

Enjoy a sophisticated dessert with these Poached Pears in Red Wine. The gentle poaching process imbues the pears with a luscious red wine reduction, intensifying their natural sweetness. Garnished with whipped cream or vanilla ice cream, it's a romantic finish to any meal.

POACHED PEARS IN RED WINE

4	ripe, firm pears
1	750 ml bottle of Pinot Noir
1 1/2	cups granulated sugar
1	vanilla bean, split lengthwise
2	cinnamon sticks
4	cloves
1	orange, zested
	Whipped cream or vanilla ice cream, for serving

Prep Time: 15 minutes
Cook Time: 50 minutes
Total Time: 1 hour, 5 minutes
Servings: 4

Peel the pears, leaving the stems intact. Slice a thin layer off the bottom of each pear to create a flat base. In a large saucepan, combine the Pinot Noir, sugar, vanilla bean, cinnamon sticks, cloves, and orange zest. Stir over medium heat until the sugar is dissolved. Place the pears upright in the saucepan. The liquid should almost cover the pears.Bring the liquid to a low boil, reduce the heat to low, and simmer for about 25-30 minutes, until the pears are tender when pierced with a knife.

Use a slotted spoon to carefully remove the pears from the saucepan. Set them aside to cool. Remove the vanilla bean, cinnamon sticks, cloves, and orange zest from the saucepan. Increase the heat to medium-high and simmer the liquid for about 15-20 minutes, until it is reduced by half and has a syrupy consistency. Pour the syrup over the pears before serving. Garnish with whipped cream or a scoop of vanilla ice cream if desired.

Wine Pairing:
This dessert pairs beautifully with a glass of the same Pinot Noir used in the recipe. The wine's earthy tones and mild tannin structure make it versatile enough to pair with a wide variety of dishes, including this subtly sweet dessert. Enjoy a glass of Pinot Noir to enhance the flavor of the poached pears and make your meal even more memorable.

Light, crisp, and decidedly decadent, this Raspberry Mille Feuille is a French pastry classic. Layers of puff pastry and creamy custard are stacked high, punctuated with tart, fresh raspberries.

RASPBERRY MILLE FEUILLE

1	package puff pastry (2 sheets), thawed
1	cup whole milk
2	large egg yolks
1/4	cup granulated sugar
1	tablespoon all-purpose flour
1	tablespoon cornstarch
1	teaspoon pure vanilla extract
1	cup heavy cream
2	tablespoons powdered sugar
1	cup fresh raspberries
	Powdered sugar, for dusting

Prep Time: 30 minutes
Cook Time: 20 minutes
Total Time: 50 minutes (plus chilling time)
Servings: 6

Preheat the oven to 400°F (200°C). Unroll the puff pastry sheets and cut each into 9 equal squares. Place the squares on a baking sheet lined with parchment paper. Bake for 15 minutes or until golden and puffed. Set aside to cool. While the pastry is baking, make the custard. Heat the milk in a medium saucepan over medium heat until it just begins to steam. Do not boil.

In a separate bowl, whisk together the egg yolks, granulated sugar, flour, and cornstarch until smooth. Slowly whisk half of the hot milk into the egg mixture, then pour the egg-milk mixture back into the saucepan with the remaining milk. Cook over medium heat, whisking constantly, until the custard thickens and comes to a slow boil. Remove from heat and stir in the vanilla extract. Transfer the custard to a bowl and cover with plastic wrap, pressing the wrap directly onto the surface of the custard to prevent a skin from forming. Chill until cool. Whip the heavy cream and powdered sugar until soft peaks form. Fold half of the whipped cream into the cooled custard.

To assemble, layer a square of puff pastry, a spoonful of custard cream, a few raspberries, another square of puff pastry, more custard cream, more raspberries, and finally a third square of puff pastry. Repeat with the remaining ingredients. Dust the assembled pastries with powdered sugar and serve with the remaining whipped cream on the side.

Wine Pairing:
Serve this exquisite dessert with a glass of Champagne Rosé. The wine's fine bubbles and delicate pink hue make it a visually appealing match, while its fresh, fruity flavor profile beautifully complements the tartness of the raspberries and the richness of the custard cream.

Our Rose Petal Panna Cotta marries the creamy elegance of classic Italian panna cotta with the romantic allure of rose petals.

ROSE PETAL PANNA COTTA

2	tablespoons cold water
1 1/4	teaspoons unflavored gelatin
2	cups heavy cream
1/3	cup granulated sugar
1	tablespoon rose water
1/2	teaspoon vanilla extract
	Edible rose petals, for garnish

Prep Time: 15 minutes
Cook Time: 10 minutes
Chill Time: 4 hours
Total Time: 4 hours, 25 minutes
Servings: 6

In a small bowl, sprinkle the gelatin over the cold water. Let sit for about 5 minutes to soften. In a medium saucepan, combine the heavy cream and sugar. Heat over medium heat, stirring until the sugar is dissolved and the cream is hot but not boiling. Remove the saucepan from the heat. Add the softened gelatin to the hot cream mixture, and stir until the gelatin is completely dissolved. Stir in the rose water and vanilla extract. Pour the mixture into six small dessert glasses or ramekins. Let cool to room temperature, then cover with plastic wrap and refrigerate until set, about 4 hours or overnight. To serve, remove the panna cotta from the refrigerator, uncover, and let sit for about 10 minutes. Garnish with edible rose petals and serve.

Wine Pairing:
Moscato d'Asti, with its aromatic, sweet, and lightly sparkling profile, makes a perfect partner for the Rose Petal Panna Cotta. The wine's natural sweetness and subtle fizz create a refreshing balance to the creamy, floral dessert. Enjoy a glass of chilled Moscato d'Asti to enhance this romantic culinary experience.

Our Strawberry Shortcake is a blissful combination of flaky biscuits, fresh strawberries, and pillowy whipped cream, exuding an irresistible charm in every bite. The freshness of the strawberries and the buttery savoriness of the biscuits make this dessert a comforting treat.

STRAWBERRY SHORTCAKE

FOR THE STRAWBERRIES:

1	pound fresh strawberries, hulled and sliced
1/4	cup granulated sugar

Prep Time: 20 minutes
Cook Time: 15 minutes
Total Time: 35 minutes
Servings: 8

FOR THE SHORTCAKES:

2	cups all-purpose flour
1/4	cup granulated sugar
1	tablespoon baking powder
1/2	teaspoon salt
1/2	cup unsalted butter, cold and cut into small pieces
2/3	cup whole milk

FOR THE WHIPPED CREAM:

1	cup heavy cream
2	tablespoons powdered sugar
1	teaspoon vanilla extract

In a large bowl, combine the strawberries and sugar. Let sit for at least 30 minutes to allow the strawberries to release their juices. Preheat your oven to 425 degrees F (220 degrees C).

In another large bowl, whisk together the flour, sugar, baking powder, and salt. Add the butter, using your fingers to rub it into the flour until the mixture resembles coarse crumbs. Pour in the milk, stirring until just combined. Drop spoonfuls of the dough onto a baking sheet lined with parchment paper, spacing them about 2 inches apart. Bake for 12-15 minutes or until golden brown.

While the shortcakes are baking, beat the heavy cream, powdered sugar, and vanilla extract together until soft peaks form. To serve, split the warm shortcakes in half. Spoon some of the strawberries with their juice onto each shortcake bottom. Top with a dollop of whipped cream, then put the shortcake tops on. Serve immediately.

Wine Pairing:
A glass of sparkling rosé, with its light, refreshing, and slightly fruity flavor, makes an excellent accompaniment to the sweet, ripe strawberries and rich, flaky shortcake. The wine's effervescence cuts through the creaminess of the dessert, making each bite even more delightful.

A classic Italian dessert, our Tiramisu is a symphony of bold flavors and contrasting textures. Layers of ladyfingers soaked in strong espresso and rich, creamy mascarpone cream, dusted with a generous amount of cocoa powder, create a dessert that is at once velvety and airy, sweet, and slightly bitter.

TIRAMISU

6	egg yolks
3/4	cup granulated sugar
2/3	cup milk
1 1/4	cups heavy cream
1/2	teaspoon pure vanilla extract
8 oz	mascarpone cheese
1	cup strong brewed espresso, cooled
2	packages ladyfingers (approximately 24 cookies)
2	tablespoons unsweetened cocoa powder

Prep Time: 30 minutes
Cook Time: 10 minutes
Rest Time: 2 - 8 hours
Total Time: 2 hours, 40 minutes -
8 hours, 40 minutes
Servings: 6

In a medium saucepan, whisk together egg yolks and sugar until well blended. Add in milk and cook over medium heat, stirring constantly until mixture boils. Boil gently for 1 minute, then remove from heat and allow to cool slightly. Cover tightly and chill in refrigerator for 1 hour.

In a medium bowl, beat heavy cream and vanilla until stiff peaks form. Beat in mascarpone into yolk mixture until smooth.

In a small dish, dip each ladyfinger into espresso for 5 seconds. Letting the cookies soak too long will cause them to fall apart. Place the soaked cookies on the bottom of a 8 inch dish. Spread half of the mascarpone mixture over the ladyfingers. Repeat with another layer of ladyfingers and mascarpone cream. Cover and refrigerate 2 to 8 hours, until set. Before serving, dust with cocoa powder using a fine mesh strainer. Serve chilled.

Wine Pairing:
A sweet and fizzy Moscato d'Asti is a beautiful partner for this Tiramisu. The light, sweet bubbles help cleanse the palate and balance the rich, creamy flavors of the dessert. The Moscato's subtle peach and apricot undertones also complement the bitterness of the espresso and cocoa wonderfully.

COCKTAILS

Aviation

2 oz   gin
1/2 oz   lemon juice
1/2 oz   maraschino liqueur
1/4 oz   1crème de violette
          Cherry and lemon twist for garnish

Servings: 1

Chill a cocktail glass by filling it with ice and letting it sit while you prepare the cocktail.

Add the gin, lemon juice, maraschino liqueur, and crème de violette to a cocktail shaker. Fill the shaker with ice and shake vigorously for about 20 seconds until well-chilled. Empty the ice from the cocktail glass and strain the mixture into the glass. Garnish with a cherry and a twist of lemon peel. Serve immediately and enjoy this classic, elegant cocktail.

The Aviation is a classic cocktail from the early 20th century. It's known for its distinctive pale sky-blue color and elegant, refreshing taste. The drink was first published in "Recipes for Mixed Drinks" by Hugo R. Ensslin in 1916, who was the head bartender at the Hotel Wallick in New York. For many years, the Aviation was almost forgotten, as crème de violette was quite hard to find. However, with its resurgence, the Aviation has reclaimed its place among the pantheon of classic cocktails. It's a smooth, sophisticated blend of gin, lemon juice, maraschino liqueur, and the elusive crème de violette that gives it a unique floral touch and the sky-blue tint.

Bloody Mary

Servings: 1

2 oz	vodka
4 oz	tomato juice
1/2 oz	lemon juice
4 dashes	Worcestershire sauce
4 dashes	hot sauce, or to taste
1 pinch	salt and pepper
	Celery stalk and lemon wedge, for garnish

Fill a shaker with ice and add the vodka, tomato juice, lemon juice, Worcestershire sauce, hot sauce, salt, and pepper. Shake vigorously until well mixed. Strain the mixture into a tall glass filled with ice. Garnish with a celery stalk and a lemon wedge. Serve immediately, with a stirring rod or straw for further mixing if desired.

The Bloody Mary is a classic cocktail known for its savory and spicy flavors, often served at brunch. The origins of the Bloody Mary are somewhat murky, with multiple bartenders claiming to have invented the cocktail. One of the most popular stories attributes its creation to Ferdinand "Pete" Petiot at Harry's New York Bar in Paris during the 1920s. The cocktail was then said to have been popularized in the United States at the St. Regis Hotel in New York City. This bold, tomato-based drink with a vodka punch can be garnished with a variety of items, making it a versatile and customizable cocktail.

Brown Derby

2 oz   bourbon   Servings: 1
1 oz   fresh grapefruit juice
1/2 oz   honey syrup (To make honey syrup, mix equal
           parts of honey and warm water until they integrate)
           Grapefruit twist, for garnish

Add bourbon, grapefruit juice, and honey syrup into a cocktail shaker filled with ice. Shake vigorously until the outside of the shaker is frosty, about 20 seconds. Strain into a chilled cocktail glass. Garnish with a twist of grapefruit.

The Brown Derby, also known as a De Rigueur in some circles, is a cocktail from the golden age of Hollywood. The drink is named after a famous Los Angeles diner that was shaped like a man's derby hat, a popular spot for movie stars in the 1930s and 1940s. This classic cocktail showcases the smooth harmony of bourbon with the fresh, bright flavors of grapefruit and honey, embodying the Hollywood glamour of yesteryears.

ESPRESSO MARTINI

2 oz	vodka	Servings: 1
1 oz	espresso or strong coffee, cooled	
1/2 oz	coffee liqueur	
1/2 oz	simple syrup	
	Coffee beans, for garnish	

Fill a cocktail shaker with ice, then add the vodka, cooled espresso or strong coffee, coffee liqueur, and simple syrup. Shake vigorously for about 20 seconds until well-chilled. Strain into a chilled martini glass. Garnish with a few coffee beans.

*The Espresso Martini is a cold, coffee-flavored cocktail made with vodka, espresso coffee, coffee liqueur, and sugar syrup. It was created in the 1980s by London bartender Dick Bradsell. The story goes that a model walked into the bar and asked for a drink that would "wake me up and then f*** me up". With its invigorating blend of vodka and coffee, the Espresso Martini was his answer. Today, it is enjoyed worldwide, often as an after-dinner drink.*

French 75

2 oz gin
1 oz fresh lemon juice
1 oz simple syrup
  Champagne, to top off
  Lemon twist, for garnish

Servings: 1

In a cocktail shaker filled with ice, combine the gin, lemon juice, and simple syrup. Shake well until chilled and well mixed. Strain into a Champagne flute. Top off with your favorite Champagne. Garnish with a lemon twist.

The French 75 is a cocktail held in such high esteem that it falls easily into the canon of classic cocktails. Originated during World War I, it was first recorded in "Harry's ABC of Mixing Cocktails" and its combination of gin, lemon juice, sugar, and Champagne is said to have such a kick that it felt like being shelled with the powerful French 75mm field gun. The cocktail offers a bubbly, refreshing citrus flavor, making it perfect for celebrations or a classy date night.

JUNGLE BIRD

1 1/2 oz dark rum
3/4 oz   Campari
1/2 oz   simple syrup
1 1/2 oz pineapple juice
1/2 oz   fresh lime juice
         Pineapple wedge or leaf, for garnish

Servings: 1

Combine rum, Campari, simple syrup, pineapple juice, and lime juice in a cocktail shaker filled with ice. Shake well until the outside of the shaker becomes frosty. Strain into a glass filled with crushed ice. Garnish with a pineapple wedge or leaf.

The Jungle Bird is a tropical cocktail created in the late 1970s at the Aviary bar of the Kuala Lumpur Hilton. This tiki-style cocktail is well-known for its unique combination of flavors—deep, dark rum paired with the bitter, citrus notes of Campari, balanced by pineapple and lime juices, and sweetened slightly with simple syrup.

Last Word

3/4 oz   gin
3/4 oz   green Chartreuse
3/4 oz   Maraschino liqueur
3/4 oz   fresh lime juice

Servings: 1

Add gin, green Chartreuse, Maraschino liqueur, and fresh lime juice into a cocktail shaker filled with ice. Shake well until the mixture is fully combined and chilled. Strain the mixture into a chilled cocktail glass. Serve immediately, no garnish is needed.

The Last Word is a Prohibition-era cocktail first mixed at the Detroit Athletic Club. The club's members loved the gin-based concoction and it gained popularity, but over time it faded into obscurity. The Last Word experienced a revival in the early 2000s, thanks to Seattle bartender Murray Stenson who found the recipe in an old bartending guide and added it to his menu.

MANHATTAN

2 oz   Rye Whiskey

1 oz   Sweet Vermouth

2 dashes Angostura Bitters

1   Maraschino Cherry (for garnish)

Servings: 1

Add the rye whiskey, sweet vermouth, and Angostura bitters into a mixing glass filled with ice. Stir well until the mixture is well-chilled. Strain the cocktail into a chilled cocktail glass. Garnish with a maraschino cherry.

The Manhattan cocktail, a classic blend of whiskey, sweet vermouth, and bitters, originated in the Manhattan Club in New York City in the 1860s. Reportedly invented for a banquet hosted by Jennie Jerome (Lady Randolph Churchill, mother of Winston Churchill), it has stood the test of time and remains a beloved drink for whiskey lovers.

Negroni Sbagliato

		Servings: 1
1 oz	Sweet Vermouth	
1 oz	Campari	
1 oz	Prosecco or other Sparkling Wine	
1	Orange Slice (for garnish)	

Fill an Old-Fashioned glass with ice cubes. Pour the sweet vermouth and Campari over the ice. Top with the Prosecco or sparkling wine. Gently stir to mix. Garnish with a slice of orange.

The Negroni Sbagliato, or "mistaken Negroni", is a delightful variation of the classic Negroni. The drink was reportedly invented at the Bar Basso in Milan, Italy, when a bartender accidentally used sparkling wine instead of gin while making a Negroni. The result was a lighter, bubblier version that was just as delicious.

WHITE RUSSIAN

2 oz	Vodka	Servings: 1
1 oz	Kahlúa (or other coffee liqueur)	
1 oz	Heavy Cream	
	Ice Cubes	

In an Old-Fashioned glass filled with ice cubes, pour the vodka and Kahlúa. Top with the heavy cream. Gently stir to mix. Some prefer to leave the cream layer on top and sip the cocktail through it.

The White Russian is a classic creamy cocktail made famous by the film "The Big Lebowski". Despite its name, it has no real connection to Russia other than its main ingredient, vodka. Its roots trace back to the 1940s when it first appeared in a Belgian publication. The cocktail earned its place in pop culture in 1998 when Jeff Bridges' character in "The Big Lebowski" adopted it as his drink of choice.

INDEX